CHOOSING
FORGIVENESS

BIBLE STUDY

Hope For The Heart Bible Studies

June Hunt

AspirePress

Hope For The Heart Bible Studies
Choosing Forgiveness Bible Study

© 2017 Hope For The Heart

Published by Aspire Press
an imprint of Hendrickson Publishing Group
Rose Publishing, LLC
P. O. Box 3473
Peabody, Massachusetts 01961-3473 USA
www.HendricksonPublishingGroup.com

ISBN 978-162862-384-0

For more information on Hope For The Heart, visit www.hopefortheheart.org or
call 1-800-488-HOPE (4673).

Printed in the United States of America
January 2021, 3rd printing

CONTENTS

About This Bible Study

THANK YOU. Sincerely. Thanks for taking the time and making the effort to invest in the study of God's Word with God's people. The apostle John wrote that he had "no greater joy than to hear that my children are walking in the truth" (3 John 4). At HOPE FOR THE HEART, our joy comes from seeing God use our materials to help His children walk in the truth.

OUR FOUNDATION

God's Word is our sure and steady anchor. We believe the Bible is *inspired* by God (He authored it through human writers), *inerrant* (completely true), *infallible* (totally trustworthy), and the *final authority* on all matters of life and faith. This study will give you *biblical* insight on the topic of forgiveness.

WHAT TO EXPECT IN THIS BIBLE STUDY

The overall flow of this topical Bible study looks at forgiveness and unforgiveness from four angles: Definitions, Characteristics, Causes, and Biblical Steps to Solution.

- The **DEFINITIONS** section orients you to the topic by laying the foundation for a broad understanding of forgiveness from a biblical and emotional standpoint. It answers the question: What does it mean?

- The **CHARACTERISTICS** section spotlights various aspects that are often associated with forgiveness and unforgiveness, giving a deeper understanding to the topic. It answers the question: What does it look like?

- The CAUSES section identifies the physical, emotional, and spiritual sources of unforgiveness. It answers the question: What causes it?

- The BIBLICAL STEPS TO SOLUTION sections provide action plans designed to help you—and help you help others— learn to forgive from a scriptural point of view. It answers the question: What can you do about it?

The individual sessions contain narrative, biblical teaching, and discussion questions for group interaction and personal application. We sought to strike a balance between engaging content, biblical truth, and practical application.

GUIDELINES

Applying the following biblical principles will help you get the most out of this Bible-based study as you seek to live a life pleasing to the Lord.

- PRAY – "Unless the LORD builds the house, the builders labor in vain" (Psalm 127:1). Any progress in spiritual growth comes from the Lord's helping hand, so soak your study in prayer. We need to depend on God's wisdom to study, think, and apply His Word to our lives.

- PREPARE – Even ants prepare and gather food in the harvest (Proverbs 6:6–8). As with most activities in life, you will get out of it as much as you put into it. You will reap what you sow (Galatians 6:7). Realize, the more you prepare, the more fruit you produce.

- PARTICIPATE – Change takes place in the context of community. Come to each session ready to ask questions, engage with others, and seek God's help. And "do everything in love" (1 Corinthians 16:14).

- PRACTICE – James says, "Do not merely listen to the word, and so deceive yourselves. Do what it says" (James 1:22). Ultimately, this Bible study is designed to impact your life.

- **PASS IT ON!** – The Bible describes a spiritual leader who "set his heart to study the Law of the LORD, and to do it and to teach his statutes and rules" (Ezra 7:10 ESV). Notice the progression: *study . . . do . . . teach*. That progression is what we want for your journey. We pray that God will use the biblical truths contained in this material to change your life and then to help you help others! In this way, the Lord's work will lead to more and more changed lives.

OUR PRAYER

At HOPE FOR THE HEART, we pray that the biblical truths within these pages will give you the hope and help you need to handle the challenges in your life. And we pray that God will reveal Himself and His will to you through this study of Scripture to make you more like Jesus. Finally, we pray that God's Spirit will strengthen you, guide you, comfort you, and equip you to live a life that honors Jesus Christ.

A Note to Group Leaders

*"Do your best to present yourself to God as one
approved, a worker who does not need to
be ashamed and who correctly handles
the word of truth."*

2 Timothy 2:15

Thank you for leading this group. Your care and commitment to the members doesn't go unnoticed by God. Through this study, God will use you to do His work: to comfort, to encourage, to challenge, and even to bring people to saving faith in Christ. For your reference, we've included a gospel message on page 12 to assist you in bringing people to Christ. The following are some helpful tips for leading the sessions.

TIPS FOR LEADERS

- **Pray** – Ask God to guide you, the members, and your time together as a group. Invite the group members to share prayer requests each week.

- **Prepare** – Look over the sessions before you lead. Familiarize yourself with the content and find specific points of emphasis for your group.

- **Care** – Show the members you are interested in their lives, their opinions, and their struggles. People will be more willing to share if you show them you care.

- **Listen** – Listen to the Lord's leading and the members' responses. Ask follow-up questions. A listening ear is often more meaningful than a good piece of advice.

- **Guide** – You don't have to "teach" the material. Your role is to *facilitate group discussion*: ask questions, clarify confusion, and engage the group members.

BEFORE THE FIRST MEETING

Schedule

- Determine the size of the group. Keep in mind that people tend to share more freely and develop genuine intimacy in smaller groups.

- Pick a time and place that works well for everyone.

- Decide how long each session will run. Sessions shouldn't take more than an hour or hour and a half.

- Gather the group members' contact information. Decide the best method of communicating (phone, text, email, etc.) with them outside of the group meeting.

Set Expectations

- CONFIDENTIALITY – Communicate that what is shared in the group needs to stay in the group.

- RESPECTFULNESS – Emphasize the importance of respecting each other's opinions, experiences, boundaries, and time.

- PRAYER – Decide how you want to handle prayer requests. If you take prayer requests during group time, factor in how much time that will take during the session. It may be more effective to gather requests on note cards during the sessions or have members email them during the week.

AT THE FIRST MEETING

Welcome

- Thank the members of your group for coming.

- Introduce yourself and allow others to introduce themselves.

- Explain the overall structure of study (Definitions, Characteristics, Causes, and Steps to Solution), including the discussion/application questions.

- Pray for God's wisdom and guidance as you begin this study.

LEADING EACH SESSION

Overview

- Summarize and answer any lingering questions from the previous session.

- Give a broad overview of what will be covered in each session.

How to Encourage Participation

- PRAY. Ask God to help the members share openly and honestly about their struggles. Some people may find it overwhelming to share openly with people they may not know very well. Pray for God's direction and that He would help build trust within the group.

- EXPRESS GRATITUDE AND APPRECIATION. Thank the members for coming and for their willingness to talk.

- **SPEAK FIRST.** The leader's willingness to share often sets the pace and depth of the group. Therefore, it is important that you, as the leader, begin the first few sessions by sharing from your own experience. This eases the pressure of the other members to be the first to talk. The group members will feel more comfortable sharing as the sessions progress. By the third or fourth session, you can ask others to share first.

- **ASK QUESTIONS.** Most of the questions in the study are open-ended. Avoid yes/no questions. Ask follow-up and clarifying questions so you can understand exactly what the members mean.

- **RESPECT TIME.** Be mindful of the clock and respectful of the members' time. Do your best to start and end on time.

- **RESPECT BOUNDARIES.** Some members share more easily than others. Don't force anyone to share who doesn't want to. Trust takes time to build.

Dealing with Difficulties

- You may not have an answer to every question or issue that arises. That's okay. Simply admit that you don't know and commit to finding an answer.

- Be assertive. Some people are more talkative than others, so it is important to limit the amount of time each person shares so everyone has a chance to speak. You can do this by saying something like: "I know this is a very important topic and I want to make sure everyone has a chance to speak, so I'm going to ask that everyone would please be brief when sharing." If someone tries to dominate the conversation, thank them for sharing, then invite others to speak. You can offer a non-condemning statement such as: "Good, thank you for sharing. Who else would like to share?" Or, "I'd like to make sure everyone has a chance to speak. Who would like to go next?"

- Sometimes people may not know how to answer a question or aren't ready to share their answer. Give the group time to think and process the material. Be okay with silence. Rephrasing the question can also be helpful.

- If someone misses a session, contact that person during the week. Let them know you noticed they weren't there and that you missed them.

WRAPPING UP

- Thank the group for their participation.

- Provide a brief summary of what the next session will cover.

- Encourage them to study the material for the next session during the week.

- Close in prayer. Thank God for the work He is doing in the group and in each person's life.

We are grateful to God for your commitment to lead this group. May God bless you as you guide His people toward the truth—truth that sets us free!

*"If [your gift] is to lead,
do it diligently."*

Romans 12:8

FOUR POINTS OF GOD'S PLAN

The gospel is central to all we do at Hope For The Heart. More than anything, we want you to know the saving love and grace of Jesus Christ. The following shows God's plan of salvation for you!

#1 GOD'S PURPOSE FOR YOU IS SALVATION.

God sent Jesus Christ to earth to express His love for you, save you, forgive your sins, empower you to have victory over sin, and to enable you to live a fulfilled life (John 3:16–17; 10:10).

#2 YOUR PROBLEM IS SIN.

Sin is living independently of God's standard—knowing what is right, but choosing what is wrong (James 4:17). The penalty of sin is spiritual death, eternal separation from God (Isaiah 59:2; Romans 6:23).

#3 GOD'S PROVISION FOR YOU IS THE SAVIOR.

Jesus died on the cross to personally pay the penalty for your sins (Romans 5:8).

#4 YOUR PART IS SURRENDER.

Place your faith in (rely on) Jesus Christ as your personal Lord and Savior and reject your "good works" as a means of earning God's approval (Ephesians 2:8–9). You can tell God that you want to surrender your life to Christ in a simple, heartfelt prayer like this: "God, I want a real relationship with You. Please forgive me for my sins. Jesus, thank You for dying on the cross to pay the penalty for my sins. Come into my life and be my Lord and Savior. In Your holy name I pray. Amen."

WHAT CAN YOU EXPECT NOW?

When you surrender your life to Christ, God empowers you to live a life pleasing to Him (2 Peter 1:3–4). Jesus assures those who believe with these words: "Very truly I tell you, whoever hears my word and believes him who sent me has eternal life and will not be judged but has crossed over from death to life" (John 5:24).

SESSION 1

DEFINITIONS OF FORGIVENESS

"Bear with each other and forgive one another if any of you has a grievance against someone. Forgive as the Lord forgave you."

Forgiveness. Something about this study has piqued your interest. Perhaps you desire a deeper biblical understanding on what forgiveness is, or maybe forgiveness is a constant challenge for you or someone you know. Right now, before you begin this study, ask God to open your heart to give you a better understanding. There is no shame in the struggle to forgive. The struggle is real.

All you have to do is take a look at history to discover others who struggled with forgiveness.

The Story of Corrie ten Boom

The year is 1944. Nazi Germany occupies Holland. An elderly watchmaker and his family are actively involved in the Dutch underground. By hiding Jewish people in a secret room of their home, members of the Ten Boom family courageously help Jewish men, women, and children escape Hitler's roll call of death.[1]

Yet one fateful day, their secret is discovered. The watchmaker is arrested, and soon after being punished, he dies. His tenderhearted daughter Betsie also dies in the Nazi concentration camp at the hands of her cruel captors. Only the watchmaker's youngest daughter, Corrie, survives one of Hitler's most horrific death camps. Will she ever be able to forgive her captors, those who caused the death of her father and her sister?

There is no shame in the struggle to forgive. The struggle is real.

Two years after the war, Corrie is speaking at a church in Munich. She has come from Holland to a defeated Germany, bringing with her the message that God does indeed forgive. There in the crowd, a solemn face stares back at her. As the people file out, a balding, heavyset man in a gray overcoat moves toward her clutching a brown felt hat. Suddenly a scene flashes back in her mind: the blue uniform, the visored cap with its skull and crossbones, the huge room with its harsh overhead lights—the humiliation of walking naked past this man . . . this man who is now standing before her.

"You mentioned Ravensbruck in your talk. I was a guard there," he says. "But since that time I have become a Christian. I know that God has forgiven me for the cruel things I did there, but I would like to hear it from your lips as well." He extends his hand toward her and asks, "Will you forgive me?"[2]

Corrie stares at the outstretched hand. The moment seems like hours as she wrestles with the most difficult decision she has ever had to make. Corrie knows Scripture well, but applying this passage seems to be too much: "If your brother or sister sins against you, rebuke them; and if they repent, forgive them. Even if they sin against you seven times in a day and seven times come back to you saying 'I repent,' you must forgive them" (Luke 17:3–4).

In this session, we'll look at various definitions of forgiveness, how forgiveness relates to reconciliation, and God's forgiveness.

Write from the Heart

What recent news stories or historical events make forgiveness seem humanly impossible?

Imagine being in Corrie's shoes when the guard from Ravensbruck approached her. How do you think you would you have responded?

What Is Forgiveness?

Imagine you need to borrow $100 to help pay a medical bill. You ask a friend for a loan and promise to pay it back at the end of the month. But when the time comes for repayment, you don't have the money. In fact, for the next three months, you still don't have the money. Then unexpectedly, out of the kindness of his heart, your friend chooses to forgive the debt! This is one facet of forgiveness.

- *Forgiveness* means dismissing a debt.[3] When you forgive someone, you dismiss the debt owed to you. When you *receive* forgiveness, *your* debt is dismissed; no repayment is required.

- *Forgiveness* is dismissing your demand that others owe you something, especially when they fail to meet your expectations, fail to keep a promise, or fail to treat you justly.

- *Forgiveness* is dismissing, canceling, or setting someone free from the consequence of falling short of God's standard.

WHAT FORGIVENESS IS NOT[4]

Misconceptions abound about forgiveness. Some mistakenly think that forgiveness is equivalent to *excusing* sin, saying that what was wrong is now right. Yet we do not find that in Scripture. In fact, when Christ encountered the mob of men eager to stone a woman caught in adultery, He did not excuse her. Instead, He said, "Go, and sin no more" (John 8:11 KJV).

- **Forgiveness is not based on what is fair.**

  It is not "fair" that Christ was crucified, but His death provided forgiveness for us.

- **Forgiveness is not circumventing God's justice.**

  It is allowing God to execute His justice in His time and in His way.

- **Forgiveness is not denying the hurt.**

  It is feeling the hurt and releasing it.

- **Forgiveness is not dependent on an apology.**

  It is possible that some people will never apologize.

- **Forgiveness is not enablement.**

  It is refusing to permit irresponsible people to continue being irresponsible.

- **Forgiveness is not excusing bad behavior.**

  It is forgiving even when the behavior is inexcusable.

- **Forgiveness is not explaining away the hurt.**

  It is working through the hurt.

- **Forgiveness is not forgetting.**

  It is necessary to remember before you can forgive.

- **Forgiveness is not repentance.**

  It is the gift of grace even though the offender is undeserving.

- **Forgiveness is not stuffing your anger.**

  It is resolving your anger by releasing the offense to God.

- **Forgiveness is not waiting for "time to heal all wounds."**

  It is clear that time doesn't heal all wounds.

- **Forgiveness is not a sign of weakness.**

  It is being strong enough to be Christlike.

- **Forgiveness is not a natural response.**

  It is a supernatural response, empowered by God.

- **Forgiveness is not a feeling.**

  It is a choice, an act of the will.

- **Forgiveness is not conditional.**

  It is a mandate from God.

Write from the Heart

After reviewing the list of what forgiveness is *not*, which of these misconceptions have impacted your understanding of forgiveness the most? In what way?

....

....

....

....

....

Read Colossians 3:13. What do you learn from this Scripture about how to handle grievances? What difficulties, if any, have you experienced doing this?

....

....

....

....

....

....

....

What Does It Mean To Forgive?

A loose woman was caught "in the act," and the stone throwers were ready. The penalty for adultery was clear—*stone the adulterers to death*! Jesus challenged the stone throwers to examine their own hearts before condemning the woman's behavior. "Let any one of you who is without sin be the first to throw a stone at her." No one moved. Then, after all the stones dropped, *one by one*, and the stone throwers left, *one by one*, Jesus focused His attention on the woman. He looked beyond her fault and saw her need. She needed to know the life-changing love of God. Jesus gave her a priceless gift—His merciful favor and forgiveness. "'Neither do I condemn you,' Jesus declared. 'Go now and leave your life of sin.'" (You can read this story in John 7:53–8:11.)

To forgive means you release your resentment toward your offender.

- You release your demand to hear "I'm sorry."

- You release your feelings of bitterness.

- You release your desire to get even.

> *"Do not repay anyone evil for evil.*
> *Be careful to do what is right*
> *in the eyes of everyone."*
>
> Romans 12:17

To forgive means you release your rights regarding the offense.

- You release your right to dwell on the wrong done to you. You think about other things.

- You release your right to hold on to the offense. You let it go.

- You release your right to keep bringing up the offense. You stop talking about it.

"Whoever would foster love covers over an offense, but whoever repeats the matter separates close friends."

PROVERBS 17:9

To forgive means you reflect the character of Christ. You are to be like Him.

- To forgive is to extend mercy. Christ is merciful to you.

- To forgive is to give a gift of grace. Christ gives you the gift of grace.

- To forgive is to set the offender free. Christ sets you free.

"Forgive us our debts, as we also have forgiven our debtors."

MATTHEW 6:12

Is Forgiveness the Same as Reconciliation?[5]

No. Forgiveness is not the same as reconciliation. Forgiveness focuses on the *offense* and reconciliation focuses on the *relationship*. Forgiveness requires no relationship. Reconciliation requires a relationship in which two people, in agreement, are walking toward the same goal.

Sometimes reconciliation may not be appropriate. Talk with a trusted pastor or counselor who can help you determine whether reconciliation is advisable in your situation.

FORGIVENESS	RECONCILIATION
Can take place with only one person.	Requires at least two persons.
Is directed one way.	Is reciprocal, occurring two ways.
Is a decision to release the offender.	Is the effort to rejoin the offender.
Is a change in thinking about the offender.	Is a change in behavior by the offender.
Is a free gift to the one who has broken trust.	Is a relationship based on restored trust.
Is extended even if it is never earned.	Is offered because it has been earned.
Is unconditional, regardless of repentance.	Is conditional, based on repentance.

Write from the Heart

Do you struggle with understanding the difference between forgiveness and reconciliation? Describe a situation where you know forgiveness is necessary but reconciliation is *not*.

Divine Forgiveness on Display

Do you sometimes struggle to forgive others? Your awareness of how much God loves you and forgives you can be the catalyst to compel you to forgive others. Then you can forgive others with the Lord's *divine forgiveness.*

> *"The Lord our God is merciful and forgiving, even though we have rebelled against him."*
> Daniel 9:9

- *Divine forgiveness* is the fact that God, in His mercy, chose to release you from the penalty of all your sins—past, present, and future.

  "As high as the heavens are above the earth, so great is his love for those who fear him; as far as the east is from the west, so far has he removed our transgressions from us" (Psalm 103:11–12).

- *Divine forgiveness* was extended by Jesus, who paid the penalty for our sins in full. He died on the cross as payment for the sins of all people. We owed a debt we could not pay. He paid a debt He did not owe.

  "But God demonstrates his own love for us in this: While we were still sinners, Christ died for us" (Romans 5:8).

- *Divine forgiveness* is an extension of grace. You are an expression of God's grace when you forgive others as He did.

  "Be kind and compassionate to one another, forgiving each other, just as in Christ God forgave you" (Ephesians 4:32).

Write from the Heart

Christ's death and resurrection makes God's forgiveness possible. It's free, and it's available to you right now. Have *you* received His forgiveness? What, if anything, is stopping you from accepting God's free gift of forgiveness *today*?

....

....

....

....

....

....

If you've already received God's forgiveness, do you ever struggle to believe that God *completely* forgives all your sins? If so, when? Why? Memorize Colossians 2:13–14 to remind yourself of God's *complete* forgiveness.

....

....

....

....

....

Maybe you're having a hard time grasping the immense forgiveness God freely extends to you. God's forgiveness is what salvation is all about. Think back to the day you decided to follow Jesus, accepting Him as the Lord and Savior of your life—the day you received His forgiveness.

God's forgiveness is what salvation is all about.

If accepting the gift of salvation and becoming a follower of Christ is something you've never done, it's not too late. The Bible says, "Today is the day of salvation" (2 Corinthians 6:2 NLT). You can place your faith and trust in Christ in the quietness of your own space. Or you can consult your Bible study leader, pastor, or another Christian to explain how you, too, can become a Christian.

"All the prophets testify about him [Jesus] that everyone who believes in him receives forgiveness of sins through his name."

ACTS 10:43

Discussion/Application Questions

1. What are some common misconceptions about forgiveness?

2. How different would your life be if you freely extended and received forgiveness? Describe the impact it would have on your relationships.

3. It's been said that Christians are the only Bible some people will ever read. What would people learn about forgiveness from the pages of your life? Where in your life do you still need to grow in order to mirror and express the forgiveness of Christ?

4. The following passages show God's forgiveness: Psalm 103:3; 130:3–4; Ephesians 1:7; Colossians 2:13–14; 1 John 1:9. Read them. Then in a written prayer, thank God for His grace and forgiveness.

Notes

Notes

"You, Lord, are forgiving and good, abounding in love
to all who call to you."
Psalms 86:5

SESSION 2

CHARACTERISTICS OF FORGIVENESS

*"Their sins and lawless acts
I will remember no more."*

HEBREWS 10:17

Standing with the Enemy: The Fight to Forgive

Here stands the enemy, the former Nazi SS officer. His very presence stands for cruelty and the stench of crematoriums at Ravensbruck. As Corrie ten Boom stares at the rough hand offered by her former captor, she knows in her head what she has to do—*forgive*. But her emotions scream silently in opposition. The very message she has been sharing with the victims of Nazi brutality emphasizes that she must forgive those who persecuted her. Forgiveness is a necessity. But Corrie stands paralyzed as the battle rages between her mind and her emotions.

Imagine Corrie's dilemma. She knows that those who have forgiven their enemies have also been able to rebuild their lives regardless of the physical horrors they suffered. But those who continue to nurse their bitterness remain imprisoned, not in Hitler's horrid concentration camps, but within their own wounded souls.

Let's face it—sometimes it is very difficult to forgive. But unforgiveness takes its toll and comes with a hefty price tag. If you keep an ever-growing list of offenses in your mind and have plans to penalize your offenders, you'll become imprisoned. When you refuse to forgive, unforgiveness keeps you emotionally attached to both the offense and the offender. To justify an unforgiving attitude, you might blame others. Though you may try to bury past hurts, they're still very much alive. The challenge is to be Christlike, even in forgiveness. "Be merciful, just as your Father is merciful" (Luke 6:36).

In this session, we'll look at the characteristics of an unforgiving heart and a forgiving heart.

Write from the Heart

Like Corrie ten Boom, many people experience barriers to forgiveness. What are some common barriers people have that make forgiveness difficult?

....

....

....

....

....

....

What barriers do you have to overcome in order to forgive someone?

....

....

....

....

....

....

Recognizing the Unforgiving Heart

The telltale signs of an unforgiving heart are often hard to hide. Even when you've forgiven an offender, you might have the tendency to take back that forgiveness, just long enough to nurse the wound one more time. When you give in and allow yourself to think about the hurt, you reopen the wound. Maybe you didn't forgive them *completely.*

As you read the following descriptions of an unforgiving heart, think about yourself and ask: Do I show any signs of an unforgiving heart?

- *The unforgiving heart* is judgmental and condemning, always thinking about or bringing up in conversation the past wrongs of the offender.

  Ask yourself: Who do I always talk about negatively?

  "Do not judge. . . . Do not condemn. . . . Forgive, and you will be forgiven" (Luke 6:37).

- *The unforgiving heart* has no mercy and is always rehearsing the reasons why the offender does not deserve mercy.

  Ask yourself: Whose sins do I keep track of?

  "Judgment without mercy will be shown to anyone who has not been merciful. Mercy triumphs over judgment" (James 2:13).

- *The unforgiving heart* is resentful and envious, begrudging or coveting the successes and accomplishments of the offender.

  Ask yourself: Who do I envy right now? Whose success threatens my own happiness?

  "Love does not envy . . . it is not . . . resentful" (1 Corinthians 13:4–5 ESV).

- *The unforgiving heart* retaliates and is vengeful. It delights when the offender fails and conspires to get even with the offender.

  Ask yourself: When I hear that my offender has failed in any way, do I feel good about it?

  "Do not gloat when your enemy falls; when they stumble, do not let your heart rejoice" (Proverbs 24:17).

- *The unforgiving heart* is slanderous and maligning. It talks to others about the faults of the offender with the intent to hurt.

  Ask yourself: When is the last time I spoke negatively about the offender I "forgave" so long ago? Has my continual telling and retelling become my life script?

  "Whoever conceals hatred with lying lips and spreads slander is a fool" (Proverbs 10:18).

- *The unforgiving heart* is haughty and prideful, acting arrogantly and elevating self above the offender.

  Ask yourself: Do I look down on the one who offended me? Does my pride cause me to rank myself higher than my offender?

  "Pride goes before destruction, a haughty spirit before a fall" (Proverbs 16:18).

- *The unforgiving heart* is profane and bitter, verbally abusive, and harbors hostility toward the offender.

  Ask yourself: Who do I curse under my breath every time they come to mind?

  "Their mouths are full of cursing and bitterness" (Romans 3:14).

- ***The unforgiving heart*** is resistant and complaining. It is quick to quarrel over the offender's personal choices, words, and deeds and refuses to change one's attitude toward the offender.

  Ask yourself: In what ways am I acting closed-minded toward my offender?

  "Do everything without grumbling or arguing" (Philippians 2:14).

- ***The unforgiving heart*** is impatient and easily annoyed, easily provoked and irritated by the offender.

  Ask yourself: Can others see that I've allowed my offender to repeatedly frustrate me? Does my life revolve around the wrong I perceive has been done to me?

  "A person's wisdom yields patience; it is to one's glory to overlook an offense" (Proverbs 19:11).

Write from the Heart

Which of the characteristics of the unforgiving heart do you see in yourself? Ask God to help you in this area.

....

....

....

....

....

....

....

Read Ephesians 4:31–32. What negative attitudes and actions *are not* to be part of your life? What positive attitudes and actions *are* to be present?

....

....

....

....

....

....

Recognizing the Forgiving Heart

The moment you entrust your life to Jesus, you are *sealed* with the Holy Spirit, who dwells within you for the rest of your life.

"You also were included in Christ when you heard the message of truth, the gospel of your salvation. When you believed, you were marked in him with a seal, the promised Holy Spirit, who is a deposit guaranteeing our inheritance until the redemption of those who are God's possession—to the praise of his glory" (Ephesians 1:13–14).

When the Spirit of Christ is rooted within you, He produces fruit consistent with the character of Christ. Just as orange trees produce oranges and banana trees produce bananas, the Spirit of Christ produces the character of Christ in a Christian. Therefore, the next time you are wronged, allow the Holy Spirit the freedom to produce His fruit of forgiveness in you.

"The fruit of the Spirit is love, joy, peace, patience, kindness, goodness, faithfulness, gentleness, self-control."

GALATIANS 5:22–23 ESV

One result of true forgiveness is peace—peace in the knowledge that you have followed Christ's example, forgiving just as He has forgiven you. Through the power of the Holy Spirit working in your life, you are equipped with the power necessary to forgive.

As you read the descriptions of what it means to have a forgiving heart, ask yourself: Do I display a forgiving heart toward others?

- *The forgiving heart* is loving and has a loving spirit. It does not keep a record of wrongdoing and allows the possibility that an offender can choose to change.

  Ask yourself: When I think of the one who offended me, can I see how God is allowing me to view them with more compassion than before?

  "[Love] keeps no record of wrongs" (1 Corinthians 13:5).

- *The forgiving heart* has a joyful awareness that God will use trials to bring triumph, and He is sovereign over all events in life, even the painful ones.

  Ask yourself: Do I approach life knowing that God is in control? Do I depend on Him in all things?

  "I will continue to rejoice, for I know that through your prayers and God's provision of the Spirit of Jesus Christ what has happened to me will turn out for my deliverance"
  (Philippians 1:18–19).

- *The forgiving heart* seeks peace that can help pave the way for reconciliation—if appropriate. Do I truly desire that my offender will one day have a changed life and then receive the peace of God?

  Ask yourself: Do I truly desire that peace and redemption will become a way of life for the one who offended me?

  "Peacemakers who sow in peace reap a harvest of righteousness" (James 3:18).

- **The forgiving heart** has a commitment to patience, waiting for God's power to change the offender's heart and a patient commitment to be sensitive to God's timing.

  Ask yourself: Do I have a habit of getting in the way of God's timing? Do I "play God," thinking my timing is better than God's timing?

  "Love is patient" (1 Corinthians 13:4).

- **The forgiving heart** is kind, looking for and acting in practical ways to express kindness.

  Ask yourself: What would it look like to be kind toward the one who wronged me?

  "Love is kind" (1 Corinthians 13:4).

- **The forgiving heart** is good, holding to moral principles and purity even in the midst of controversy, reflecting the highest moral character—the character of Christ.

  Ask yourself: Do I maintain integrity when times get tough? Do I reflect the love of Christ during difficult times?

  'Love must be sincere. Hate what is evil; cling to what is good. . . . Do not be overcome by evil, but overcome evil with good" (Romans 12:9, 21).

- **The forgiving heart** is faithful, praying that those who have caused such pain might have changed lives.

  Ask yourself: When is the last time I prayed for my enemy, for the one who wronged me?

  "Bless those who curse you, pray for those who mistreat you" (Luke 6:28).

- *The forgiving heart* is gentle, taking into account the woundedness of the offender and responding to harshness with a calm gentleness, understanding that often "hurt people hurt people."

  Ask yourself: Without God's grace in my life, can I see how I may have acted just as my offender acted?

  "A gentle answer turns away wrath, but a harsh word stirs up anger" (Proverbs 15:1).

- *The forgiving heart* is self-controlled, deciding ahead of time how to have a Christlike response when conflict arises.

  Ask yourself: When someone wrongs me, do I seek to act like Christ or do I react explosively, lose control, or devise a counter attack?

  "God gave us a spirit not of fear but of power and love and self-control" (2 Timothy 1:7 ESV).

Write from the Heart

Which characteristics of the forgiving heart are evident in your life?
Which ones need to be developed more?

Discussion/Application Questions

1. What do you consider to be the biggest difference between a forgiving heart and an unforgiving heart?

2. In what ways have you seen an unforgiving heart affect an individual and their relationships? How about when someone has a forgiving heart?

3. As you consider what an unforgiving heart and forgiving heart look like, what habits do you need to begin, change, or stop in order to develop a more forgiving heart?

....

....

....

....

....

....

....

4. Jesus commands us, "pray for those who mistreat you" (Luke 6:28). For some, that may seem to be a tall order. Ask God to reveal to you what to pray for the one who has wronged you. Ask Him for wisdom about how forgiveness needs to play out in your situation. Write your thoughts out as a prayer to God.

....

....

....

....

....

....

Notes

Notes

"*You, Lord, are forgiving and good, abounding in love
to all who call to you.*"
Psalms 86:5

SESSION 3

CAUSES OF UNFORGIVENESS

"For he has rescued us from the dominion of darkness and brought us into the kingdom of the Son he loves, in whom we have redemption, the forgiveness of sins."

COLOSSIANS 1:13–14

The Betrayal of a "Friend"

Amazingly the Ten Boom's little home became the hub of the underground network. From their secret hiding place, the fingers of the underground reached into the farthest corners of Holland. As those of the Ten Boom family lived their double lives, they shuffled the hunted Jews into their one-room hiding place for sometimes up to two weeks, while members of the underground sought to slip the stowaways out of the country to safety.

Meanwhile, Corrie lived with the constant fear that they would be caught—and with reason. The family was betrayed by a fellow watchmaker whom Corrie's father had trained a few years earlier. As a result of this treachery, Corrie could never again embrace her father and she could never again delight in the presence of her beloved sister Betsie.

How could Corrie not be consumed with bitterness toward this "friend" who betrayed them? She suffered the severity of these words: "Even my close friend, someone I trusted, one who shared my bread, has turned against me" (Psalm 41:9).

No one has to tell you that forgiveness doesn't come easy. In fact, during childhood, forgiveness may have never been modeled for you in your family. Perhaps your family members held grudges. Or maybe you faced situations in your childhood that you have determined are unforgivable.

In this session, we'll look at the causes of unforgiveness, barriers to forgiveness, and the foundation of forgiveness.

Write from the Heart

As a child, were you taught to forgive? What messages (directly or indirectly) did you receive from family members about forgiveness?

Read Luke 6:27–41. What practical wisdom do you find here that relates to forgiveness? Write down an example or two you could use to teach a child to recognize both the *need* to ask for forgiveness and the *responsibility* of extending forgiveness.

Why Is Forgiving So Difficult?

There are many reasons why forgiveness is difficult. See if you identify with any of the following barriers that keep people from pursuing forgiveness.[6]

- **No modeling of forgiveness from parents**

  "I was never shown how to forgive."

- **Denying that the offense ever occurred**

  "I don't want to think about it."

- **Fearing to hold the guilty accountable**

  "It's really all my fault. I don't want to place the blame on others."

- **Not receiving forgiveness for your past offenses**

  "They didn't forgive me, so why should I forgive them?"

- **Not understanding God's forgiveness**

  "God will never forgive me, so I will never forgive her."

- **Believing that bitterness is a required response to betrayal**

  "God wouldn't allow me to feel bitter unless it was normal to feel that way."

- **Thinking that forgiveness excuses unjust behavior**

  "I'm not about to say that what she did was okay!"

- **Requiring an apology or show of repentance**

  "If he's not really sorry, he should not be forgiven."

- **Feeling a sense of power by hanging on to unforgiveness**

  "He needs to see how wrong he is!"

- **Wanting to get revenge**

  "He should pay for what he's done."

- **Harboring a prideful, hardened heart that becomes a spiritual stronghold**

  "I refuse to forgive."

"Blessed is the one who fears the LORD always, but whoever hardens his heart will fall into calamity."

PROVERBS 28:14 ESV

Write from the Heart

We all have barriers to forgiveness. Which barriers from the list do you identify with that cause you to avoid or delay extending forgiveness?

Whenever you face a barrier to forgiveness, remember the promises and forgiveness God extends to you. Read Psalm 103:8–12; Isaiah 41:10; Micah 7:19. What does God promise in these passages? How do His promises encourage you to overcome your barriers to forgiveness?

....

....

....

....

....

....

....

....

....

....

....

....

....

"I, even I, am he who blots out your transgressions, for my own sake, and remembers your sins no more."

Isaiah 43:25

Our Need for Justice

When justice is denied, we feel outraged. The cry for justice is common to everyone—except the guilty person waiting to receive justice. Then the cry is not for justice, but for *mercy*. Why is the need for justice so strong and natural, while forgiveness is so difficult and unnatural?

* God has instilled within every human heart a sense of *right* and *wrong*; therefore, we feel a need for justice when we are wronged.

* Based on the law, forgiveness seems inappropriate and unnatural.

* Because God is a God of justice, *somebody has to pay*. That Somebody was Jesus. The death of Jesus on the cross fulfilled the justice of God. In the same way that God needed to have His justice satisfied by Jesus' death, we often expect justice to be served before we extend mercy and forgiveness.

"For God presented Jesus as the sacrifice for sin. People are made right with God when they believe that Jesus sacrificed his life, shedding his blood. This sacrifice shows that God was being fair when he held back and did not punish those who sinned in times past, for he was looking ahead and including them in what he would do in this present time. God did this to demonstrate his righteousness, for he himself is fair and just, and he makes sinners right in his sight when they believe in Jesus" (Romans 3:25–26 NLT).

Write from the Heart

As simply as you can, describe the difference between *mercy* and *justice*. Describe a time when you wanted mercy and a time when you wanted justice.

....

....

....

....

....

....

....

Read James 2:13. In ten words or less, summarize what you understand this verse to mean.

....

....

....

....

....

....

The Root Cause of Unforgiveness

Everyone has been created with three God-given needs—the needs for love, significance, and security.[7] Many people who have been hurt feel insignificant and powerless. Therefore, they try to get their need for significance met by withholding forgiveness. Unforgiveness gives them a sense of power and superiority.

If you were ever betrayed by a friend, you may have felt powerless to stop the pain. Since no one likes to feel powerless, unforgiveness provides an illusion of power. By refusing to forgive, you feel a sense of power. By holding on to hatred, you feel infused with strength. By retaliating with revenge, you carry out a power play.

WRONG BELIEF	RESULT
"It's natural for me to resent those who have wronged me. If I forgive them, they will get away with it. My offenders need to pay for the wrongs committed against me."	This belief reflects an attitude of pride that sets you up as a judge higher than God Himself—God, who is willing to forgive and forget.

RIGHT BELIEF	RESULT
"Because God has totally forgiven me, I can release my resentment and choose to forgive others. I will rely on Christ, who is living within me, to forgive through me."	This belief reflects a heart of humility that results in a desire to forgive others in the same way God forgives you.

The Foundation of Forgiveness

There are many causes that can contribute to an unforgiving heart. There are many difficult barriers that can derail forgiveness. While these struggles are real, remember that forgiveness is possible because of Christ.

The Bible is not silent on the subject of forgiveness. In fact, the beautiful gospel story is painted on a canvas of mercy and forgiveness. Within all 66 books of the Bible, the sinful nature of humankind and the need for forgiveness is easily traced.

The gospel story is painted on a canvas of mercy and forgiveness.

To understand the fullness of forgiveness and to battle unforgiveness, you must continually come back to the Bible to discover its truths. The following four biblical truths will help you do just that.

1. **EVERY SIN, WITHOUT EXCEPTION, IS COVERED.**

   "If we confess our sins, he is faithful and just and will forgive us our sins and purify us from all unrighteousness" (1 John 1:9).

2. **GOD'S GRACE EXCEEDS EVERY OFFENSE.**

   "In him we have redemption through his blood, the forgiveness of sins, in accordance with the riches of God's grace" (Ephesians 1:7).

3. **FORGIVENESS IS AVAILABLE TO ALL.**

   "Everyone who believes in him [Jesus] receives forgiveness of sins through his name" (Acts 10:43).

4. **JESUS' SACRIFICE WAS ENOUGH.**

   "But when this priest [Jesus] had offered for all time one sacrifice for sins, he sat down at the right hand of God . . . For by one sacrifice he has made perfect forever those who are being made holy" (Hebrews 10:12, 14).

Discussion/Application Questions

1. What are some common reasons that people find it difficult to forgive?

....

....

....

....

....

....

....

2. Who in your life modeled forgiveness in a memorable way? How did they do it? What can you learn from their example?

....

....

....

....

....

....

....

3. Read Psalm 32:1–5, a psalm of confession. How did David feel before and after his confession? What do you learn about confession and forgiveness from this psalm?

4. Is there anyone you need to apologize to and from whom you need to ask forgiveness? (It could be for something recent or from the distant past.) Whether big or small, write out what you need to say to seek forgiveness from that person.

5. Spend a moment in silent confession, writing out any sin or
    struggles you've been dealing with lately. As you confess,
    remember that God completely forgives you (1 John 1:9).

Notes

"*You, Lord, are forgiving and good, abounding in love to all who call to you.*"

Psalms 86:5

BIBLICAL STEPS TO SOLUTION
PART 1

"God was reconciling the world to himself in Christ, not counting people's sins against them. And he has committed to us the message of reconciliation."

2 CORINTHIANS 5:19

Drawing from God Each Day

After surviving the suffering of concentration camps (living in flea and rat-infested barracks, losing her father and sister to inhumane treatment, facing death on a daily basis herself, and coping with what seemed to be the triumph of evil), life for Corrie should be basically easy—or one would assume. Wouldn't future problems pale in comparison to the horrors of her past? But by Corrie's own admission, she could not sleep at night—at least not until she made the determined decision to *choose* forgiveness on a daily basis and then to act on that decision each day. Corrie's admission is amazingly honest.

> I wish I could say that after a long and fruitful life, traveling the world, I had learned to forgive all my enemies. I wish I could say that merciful and charitable thoughts just naturally flowed from me and on to others. But they don't. If there is one thing I have learned . . . it's that I can't store up good feelings and behavior—but only draw them fresh from God each day.[8]

Corrie ten Boom learned that she not only needed to be forgiven by God, but also that she needed to forgive as God forgives. She needed to show mercy, for Jesus said . . .

"Go and learn what this means: 'I desire mercy, not sacrifice.' For I have not come to call the righteous, but sinners."

MATTHEW 9:13

In this session, we'll look at why we should forgive, how to truly forgive, and the four stages of forgiveness.

Write from the Heart

What would the world look like if everyone practiced daily forgiveness? What would the impact be on nations, marriages, parents and children, places of employment? How would *your* world look different?

....

....

....

....

....

....

....

....

....

....

....

....

....

Why Should You Forgive?

The last session covered the causes, or reasons, why it can be difficult to forgive. While there are barriers to forgiveness, there are also many biblical reasons why you should always strive to be forgiving.

You must forgive because . . .

- **God forgives you.**

  "Be kind and compassionate to one another, forgiving each other, just as in Christ God forgave you" (Ephesians 4:32).

- **God commands it.**

  "Bear with each other and forgive one another if any of you has a grievance against someone. Forgive as the Lord forgave you" (Colossians 3:13).

- **God wants you to have a heart of mercy.**

  "Blessed are the merciful, for they will be shown mercy" (Matthew 5:7).

- **God wants you to do your part to live at peace with everyone.**

  "If it is possible, as far as it depends on you, live at peace with everyone" (Romans 12:18).

- **God strengthens your witness for Christ through forgiveness.**

  "Let us not love with words or speech but with actions and in truth" (1 John 3:18).

- **God overcomes evil with good when you forgive.**

  "Do not be overcome by evil, but overcome evil with good" (Romans 12:21).

- **God stops Satan's influence when you forgive.**

  "Anyone you forgive, I also forgive. And what I have forgiven—if there was anything to forgive—I have forgiven in the sight of Christ for your sake, in order that Satan might not outwit us. For we are not unaware of his schemes" (2 Corinthians 2:10–11).

- **God brings peace through forgiveness.**

  "Whatever you have learned or received or heard from me, or seen in me—put it into practice. And the God of peace will be with you" (Philippians 4:9).

---

*Always strive
to be forgiving.*

How Do You Truly Forgive?

Have you ever said, "I was severely wronged by someone I once trusted. People want me to forgive, but how can I simply let my offender off the hook?" If these words have passed your lips or even rolled around in your mind, be assured that you are not alone. That is precisely why you need to know how to handle "the hook."

How to Handle the Hook

- Make a list of all the offenses caused by your offender.

- Imagine right now that a hook is attached to your collarbone. Then imagine all the pain attached to the hook as a result of the wrong that was done to you.

- Ask yourself, "Do I really want to carry all that pain with me for the rest of my life?" The Lord wants you to take the pain from the past and release it into His hands.

- Then take the one who offended you off your emotional hook and place your offender onto God's hook. The Lord knows how to deal with your offender in His time and in His way. God says, "It is mine to avenge; I will repay" (Deuteronomy 32:35).

- Pray the following prayer to forgive and release your offender: "Lord, You know the pain I've felt because of _____ (list every offense). I release all that pain into Your hands. Thank You for forgiving my sins. I choose to forgive _____ (name). I move _____ (name) off of my emotional hook to Your hook. I refuse all thoughts of revenge, trusting that in Your time and in Your way You will deal with _____ (name) as You see fit. Thank You for giving me Your power to forgive so I can be set free. In Jesus' name I pray. Amen."

The Four Stages of Forgiveness

Have you ever noticed that the word *forgiveness* has the little word *give* in it? When you choose to forgive, you give someone a gift—the gift of freedom from having to pay the penalty for wronging you and the gift of dismissing the debt owed to you.

Because this can be a difficult gift to give, you may need to travel through four stages of forgiveness. But realize that you are also giving yourself a gift—the gift of grudge-free living. That is true freedom.

> *"Do not seek revenge or bear a grudge against anyone among your people, but love your neighbor as yourself."*
>
> LEVITICUS 19:18

STAGE 1: FACE THE OFFENSE.

When you feel pain that is *personal*, *unfair*, and *deep*, you have a wound that can be healed only by forgiving the one who wounded you. First you must face the truth of what has actually been done. Don't hinder true healing by rationalizing or false thinking.

- **Don't excuse the offender's behavior by thinking**: "He doesn't mean to hurt me. I shouldn't feel upset with him because he's a member of my family."

  Truth: No matter the age of the offender or your relationship to them, you need to call sin, "sin." Face the truth instead of trying to change it. There must first be a guilty party in order to have someone to forgive.

"Whoever says to the guilty, 'You are innocent,' will be cursed by peoples and denounced by nations" (Proverbs 24:24).

- **Don't minimize the offense by thinking**: "No matter how badly he treats me, it's okay."

  Truth: Bad treatment is *not* okay. There is no excuse for bad treatment of any kind—any time.

  "Have nothing to do with the fruitless deeds of darkness, but rather expose them" (Ephesians 5:11).

Write from the Heart

How did that make you feel? Do you tend to minimize your own pain? If so, what are some reasons you downplay your feelings?

STAGE 2: FEEL THE OFFENSE.[9]

Christian author Lewis Smedes writes, "When a person destroys what our commitment and our intimacy created, something precious is destroyed."[10] Anger or even hatred may be your true feeling in response to deep, unfair pain. Hatred toward an offender needs to be brought up out of the basement of your soul and dealt with. However, not all hatred is wrong. God *hates* evil.

"There is a time for everything, and a season for every activity under the heavens . . . a time to love and a time to hate."

ECCLESIASTES 3:1, 8

Failing to feel the offense results in . . .

- **Denying your pain:** "I don't blame her for always criticizing me. She is under a lot of pressure, and it doesn't hurt me."

  Truth: Being mistreated by someone you love is painful. Feeling the pain must take place before healing can take place.

  "The LORD is close to the brokenhearted and saves those who are crushed in spirit" (Psalm 34:18).

- **Carrying false guilt:** "I feel guilty if I hate what was done to me. I'm never supposed to have hatred."

  Truth: God hates sin. You are to hate the sin, but not the sinner.

  "To fear the LORD is to hate evil; I hate pride and arrogance, evil behavior and perverse speech" (Proverbs 8:13).

STAGE 3: FORGIVE THE OFFENDER.

God calls you to forgive. When you do forgive, genuine forgiveness draws you into the heart of God, and your life takes on the character of Christ.

ARGUMENT	ANSWER
"I don't think it is right to forgive when I don't feel like forgiving."	Forgiveness is not a feeling, but a choice. *Read Matthew 6:12.*
"I can forgive everyone else, but I don't have the power to forgive that person."	The issue is not your lack of power to forgive, but rather how strong God's power is within you to forgive any sin committed against you. *Read 2 Peter 1:3.*
"Forgiveness isn't fair. She ought to pay for her wrong."	God knows how to deal with each person fairly—and He will, in His own time. *Read Romans 12:19.*
"I can't keep forgiving—he keeps doing the same thing over and over."	You cannot control what others do, but you can control how you respond to what others do. *Read Matthew 18:21–22.*
"I cannot forgive and forget. I keep thinking about being hurt."[11]	When you choose to forgive, you don't get a case of *holy amnesia*. After facing the hurt and confronting the offender, close your mind to rehearsing the pain of the past. *Read Philippians 3:13–14.*

Write from the Heart

Which of the "arguments" mentioned in Stage 3 do you struggle
with? Look up the corresponding Bible verse and write (in your own
words) what God says about that argument.

STAGE 4: FIND ONENESS IF APPROPRIATE.

Relationships filled with resentment ultimately perish. Relationships filled with forgiveness ultimately prevail. However, reconciliation in a relationship—the restoration of oneness—is contingent on several factors. These factors will be discussed more thoroughly in the next session. But recall from session one that reconciliation is about restoring the relationship. Reconciliation may not always be safe or appropriate, as is the case in reconciling with an abuser. Seek God's Word and talk with a pastor or counselor if you are wondering whether or not reconciliation is appropriate in your particular situation.

Generally, when both parties are committed to following biblical guidance for reconciliation and are committed to honesty in the relationship, there is real hope that the two can be of one mind and one heart again.[12]

The Bible says . . .

*"If you have any encouragement
from being united with Christ,
if any comfort from his love,
if any common sharing in the Spirit,
if any tenderness and compassion,
then make my joy complete
by being like-minded,
having the same love,
being one in spirit and of one mind."*

PHILIPPIANS 2:1–2

Discussion/Application Questions

1. Describe the differences between what the Bible tells you to do when someone wrongs you, and what your upbringing or today's culture tells you to do. How do they both influence your understanding and practice of forgiveness?

   ....

   ....

   ....

   ....

   ....

   ....

   ....

   ....

2. Read Romans 12. Choose three specific instructions in this passage that can help you exercise a forgiving spirit on a daily basis. Explain why you chose those three.

   (1) ....

   ....

   ....

   ....

(2) ....

....

....

....

(3) ....

....

....

....

3. Every day we are presented with opportunities to forgive. As you think about your day, who are the people you regularly interact with? What daily opportunities do you have to be forgiving?

....

....

....

....

....

....

....

....

....

4. You may be thinking, "Forgiving others is nearly impossible for me." Or you may feel frustrated when you see others who are quick to forgive.

In John 15:5, Jesus explains our source of help: "I am the vine; you are the branches. If you remain in me and I in you, you will bear much fruit; apart from me you can do nothing."

How does a believer remain in Christ? What daily disciplines contribute to that end? Write out a simple plan to help you abide in Christ. Ask God to help you faithfully follow the plan.

Notes

"You, Lord, are forgiving and good, abounding in love
to all who call to you."
Psalms 86:5

BIBLICAL STEPS TO SOLUTION
PART 2

"If it is possible, as far as it depends on you, live at peace with everyone. Do not take revenge, my dear friends, but leave room for God's wrath, for it is written: 'It is mine to avenge; I will repay,' says the Lord."

ROMANS 12:18–19

Forgiveness and Reconciliation

Romans 12:18–19. What a rich passage of Scripture! Read it again. The words "If it is possible, as far as it depends on you . . ." give us a glimpse of the difference between forgiveness and reconciliation. Forgiveness of others is separate from being reconciled to others. And as has already been discussed in this study, forgiveness and reconciliation are *not* the same thing. *Forgiveness* requires no relationship—it focuses on the offense. *Reconciliation* requires a relationship in the direction of the same goal. But reconciliation is not always possible.

While it would be ideal for reconciliation to follow forgiveness, reconciliation is not always the safe or sensible road to take. As previously mentioned, situations where reconciliation is not appropriate might include: reconciling with an abuser, two people involved in an adulterous affair, rape, murder, or even spiritual abuse. For some offenses, reconciliation may not be wise or safe. With that caveat in place, ask God for His direction in the decisions you make beyond forgiveness.

In this session, we'll look at how to take steps toward reconciliation and how to guard against bitterness.

"Guide me in your truth and teach me,
for you are God my Savior,
and my hope is in you all day long."

PSALM 25:5

Write from the Heart

Is there anyone you are considering reconciling with? What concerns do you have about doing so?

Steps To Reconcile

In those cases where God is impressing on your heart to seek reconciliation, the process needs to be approached wisely, under the careful leading of the Holy Spirit.

1. **Before attempting to reconcile, first seek God's counsel in His Word, in prayer, and with trusted Christians.**

   Talk with a pastor or counselor about the situation and how to best proceed. Consider having another individual present when meeting with the offender.

   "For the LORD gives wisdom; from his mouth come knowledge and understanding" (Proverbs 2:6).

2. **Honestly evaluate yourself and your relationship.**

   God intends to use your relationships to reveal your weaknesses and to strengthen your relationship with Him. Honestly evaluate your own weaknesses and the weaknesses within the relationship so that you can know where change needs to take place.

   "Search me, God, and know my heart; test me and know my anxious thoughts. See if there is any offensive way in me, and lead me in the way everlasting" (Psalm 139:23–24).

3. **Open your heart and share your pain.**

   Write a letter or have a candid conversation with the one who offended you. Don't attack your offender. Instead, address the offense and fully explain the pain you have suffered.

   "If your brother or sister sins, go and point out their fault, just between the two of you. If they listen to you, you have won them over" (Matthew 18:15).

4. **See if the offender takes responsibility for their actions.**

Offenders need to know that what they did struck like an arrow in your heart. They need to feel your hurt. If offenders ignore your pain and respond with how much you have hurt them, they are not ready for reconciliation because they are not ready to take responsibility. They need to care about your pain as much as they care about their own pain. They need to indicate a godly sorrow.

"Godly sorrow brings repentance that leads to salvation and leaves no regret, but worldly sorrow brings death" (2 Corinthians 7:10).

5. **Expect your offender to be completely truthful.**

Let the offender know that you desire honesty, support, and loyalty within the relationship. Ask if they can commit to this in the relationship going forward. Although you cannot guarantee someone else's dependability, you should be able to discern whether there is sincerity and truthfulness.

"Truthful lips endure forever, but a lying tongue lasts only a moment" (Proverbs 12:19).

6. **Set appropriate boundaries.**

You may have a heart for reconciliation. However, you need to evaluate if your offender crossed the line regarding what is appropriate (excessively angry, possessive, demeaning, insensitive, irresponsible, prideful, abusive)? If so, explain what the boundary line is, what the repercussion is for crossing the boundary (a limited relationship), and what the reward is for staying within the boundary (increased trust). You need to be firm enough to hold your offender accountable, and your offender needs to become responsible enough to stop hurting the relationship.

"Whoever heeds discipline shows the way to life, but whoever ignores correction leads others astray" (Proverbs 10:17).

7. **Take time, cautiously think, and sincerely pray before you let the offender back into your heart and life.**

When trust has been trampled, time, integrity, and consistency are needed to prove that your offender is now trustworthy. Change takes time. Therefore, don't rush the relationship. Confidence is not regained overnight. Trust is not given; it is earned.

"Above all else, guard your heart, for everything you do flows from it" (Proverbs 4:23).

8. **Yield your heart to starting over.**

God wants you to have a heart that is yielded to His perfect will for your life. Serious offenses will reshape your future, and you will not be able to come back together with your offender as though nothing ever happened. You personally change through pain. You take on new roles. You cannot simply abandon your new place in life the moment a friend is forgiven and is invited back into your heart and life. Leave negative patterns in the past and establish positive patterns of relating.

"Forget the former things; do not dwell on the past. See, I am doing a new thing! Now it springs up; do you not perceive it? I am making a way in the wilderness and streams in the wasteland" (Isaiah 43:18–19).

How to Forgive . . . Again

If you're like many, the struggle is not about whether to forgive; the struggle is the repetitive and continual need to forgive. Forgiving again and again can become discouraging. It seems about the time you've forgiven the one who wronged you, another offense is repeated, and you're faced with forgiving *again*.

While you cannot control what others do, you can control how you respond to what they do. Jesus said you are to respond with forgiveness no matter the number of times wronged (Matthew 18:21–22). Think about your relationship with God. He forgives all your sins (Colossians 2:13). God's forgiveness shows that forgiveness is not an intermittent deed—it's a permanent attitude.

The following steps show how you can maintain an attitude of forgiveness.

- **Give the situation to God.**

    When Jesus was persecuted, He knew that the heavenly Father was the final judge, judging in His way and in His time.

    "When they hurled their insults at him, he did not retaliate; when he suffered, he made no threats. Instead, he entrusted himself to him who judges justly" (1 Peter 2:23).

- **Refrain from rehearsing the wrong.**

    Stop the thoughts as soon as they enter your mind. Say to yourself, "I refuse to keep a record of this. I refuse to keep a ledger."

    "[Love] keeps no record of wrongs" (1 Corinthians 13:5).

- **Don't bring up the matter again.**

  After an honest confrontation with the offender and both sides of the situation have been dealt with—or if the other person refuses to talk about the problem—give time for the Holy Spirit to do His work of conviction.

  "Set a guard over my mouth, Lord; keep watch over the door of my lips" (Psalm 141:3).

- **Allow God's perspective to change your perspective.**

  Let God's Word to permeate your heart. During times of testing, read His Word and pray that you will reflect His love that covers over all wrongs.

  "Hatred stirs up conflict, but love covers over all wrongs" (Proverbs 10:12).

- **Intercede on behalf of your offender.**

  When you have been wronged, pray. Pray for God to help you understand your offender's past and how their inner pain has contributed to the injury you are now experiencing.

  "Far be it from me that I should sin against the Lord by failing to pray for you" (1 Samuel 12:23).

- **Show God's compassion by extending forgiveness.**

  Forgiveness is a direct expression of God's grace and mercy. Remember, *grace* is getting what you don't deserve (pardon) and *mercy* is not getting what you do deserve (punishment).

  "The Lord is full of compassion and mercy" (James 5:11).

Write from the Heart

Why do people sometimes like to keep a record of others' mistakes? How does this habit fail to reflect Christ?

Guard Against Bitterness

Jesus said, "Love your enemies." *Impossible! Unrealistic! People can't love their enemies!* At least that's the assumption. Yet the Greek word *agape*, translated "love" in this passage, means "a commitment to seek the 'highest good' for another person."[13] The "highest good" for those who are genuinely *wrong* is that their hearts become genuinely *right*. The highest good for you and me is to become followers of Christ. Indeed, His whole reason for coming to earth was to provide a way of salvation. You are to love your enemies like Christ did. You are to pray for those who persecute you just as Christ prayed for those who persecuted Him.

> *"Love your enemies and pray for those who persecute you."*
>
> Matthew 5:44

You might be thinking, "But they really aren't enemies." It's important to realize that if someone evokes resentment, bitterness, or hatred, that person is an enemy to your spirit. Because Christ commands—not suggests—that you pray for those who hurt you, you are to be obedient in doing so, knowing that praying for your enemy will help protect your heart from bitterness.

How To Pray for Those Who Hurt You

The Holy Spirit indwells every follower of Christ. As you strive to be like Christ, one approach to use in praying for your "enemy" is to pray the description of the fruit of the Spirit.

"The fruit of the Spirit is
love, joy, peace, patience, kindness, goodness,
faithfulness, gentleness, and self-control."

GALATIANS 5:22–23 ESV

Write your offender's name in the blanks below and then pray each of these prayers to the Lord.

"Lord, I pray that _____ will be filled with **love** by becoming fully aware of Your unconditional love, and in turn will be able to love others."

"Lord, I pray that _____ will be filled with **joy** because of experiencing Your joy, and in turn will radiate that inner joy to others."

"Lord, I pray that _____ will be filled with **peace**, Your inner peace that passes all understanding."

"Lord, I pray that _____ will be filled with **patience** because of experiencing Your patience, and in turn will extend that same extraordinary patience to others."

"Lord, I pray that _____ will be filled with the fruit of **kindness** because of experiencing Your kindness, and in turn will extend that same undeserved kindness to others."

"Lord, I pray that _____ will be filled with **goodness** because of experiencing the genuine goodness of Jesus, and in turn will reflect the moral goodness of Jesus to others."

"Lord, I pray that _____ will be filled with **faithfulness** because of realizing Your amazing faithfulness, and in turn will desire to be faithful to you, to Your Word, and to others."

"Lord, I pray that _____ will be filled with the fruit of **gentleness** because of experiencing Your gentleness, and in turn will be able to be gentle with others."

"Lord, I pray that _____ will be filled with **self-control**—the control by Christ of self—and in turn will rely on His control for enablement to break out of bondage and to be an example to others."

"The wisdom that comes from heaven is first of all pure; then peace-loving, considerate, submissive, full of mercy and good fruit, impartial and sincere."

JAMES 3:17

Write from the Heart

Has bitterness been a struggle for you? If so, confess your struggle to the Lord. Write a prayer asking for the Holy Spirit to empower you to overcome your bitterness and to be able to pray for those who have harmed you.

Discussion/Application Questions

1. What would be the impact on your life if you regularly practiced both forgiveness and reconciliation in your relationships?

2. Have you ever reconciled with—or attempted to reconcile with—a friend or family member who wronged you? What did you learn from that experience?

3. The tendency to blame others has been evident since the fall of man. Adam blamed Eve. Eve blamed the serpent. Why do people tend to blame others for their own wrongs instead of acknowledging their faults? Describe a time when you blamed someone else, whether openly or inwardly, for your wrong actions. What was the result?

4. Read Ephesians 4:31–5:2. What instructions do you find here? Describe a time when you knew God was nudging you to release your bitterness toward someone or apologize to someone, but you delayed doing so or completely avoided it. How did you feel during that time? What did you finally do in the end and what was the result? What could you have done differently to handle the situation better?

Notes

"*You, Lord, are forgiving and good, abounding in love
to all who call to you.*"

Psalms 86:5

BIBLICAL STEPS TO SOLUTION
PART 3

*"Blessed are the merciful, for
they will be shown mercy."*

MATTHEW 5:7

"Help Me Forgive Him"

There Corrie stands, in church, face to face with her enemy, a former Nazi SS officer. The horrors of World War II are far behind her, but the horrors of the war between forgiveness and unforgiveness still rage. How can she find the strength to take the hand of someone who represents the evil regime that destroyed the two people she held most dear? How can she forgive this man? To Corrie's dismay, she discovers she cannot:

> His hand was thrust out to shake mine. And I, who had preached so often the need to forgive, kept my hand at my side.

> Even as the angry, vengeful thoughts boiled through me, I saw the sin of them. Jesus Christ had died for this man; was I going to ask for more? Lord Jesus, I prayed, forgive me and help me to forgive him.

> I tried to smile. I struggled to raise my hand. I could not. I felt nothing, not the slightest spark of warmth or charity. And so again I breathed a silent prayer. Jesus, I cannot forgive him. Give me Your forgiveness.

> As I took his hand, the most incredible thing happened. From my shoulder along my arm and through my hand a current seemed to pass from me to him, while into my heart sprang a love for this stranger that almost overwhelmed me.

> And so I discovered that it is not on our forgiveness any more than on our goodness that the world's healing hinges, but on His. When He tells us to love our enemies, He gives along with the command, the love itself.[14]

Jesus would never tell you to "love your enemies, do good to those who hate you" (Luke 6:27) without giving you the power to do it. And Corrie ten Boom was living proof of this love until her death in 1983.

Perhaps no words reflect Corrie's heart of forgiveness and life of love more than these:

"My friends, I want you to know that through Jesus the forgiveness of sins is proclaimed to you."

Acts 13:38

Corrie's story speaks volumes about forgiveness. As this study wraps up, you will look at two stories from Scripture. The first is that of Joseph, a man who extended forgiveness. The second story is of another man, who received forgiveness yet failed to extend it. As you read through and think about these stories, consider what you would do if you were the characters in the stories. Consider how each story points to Christ.

Write from the Heart

Read through Corrie ten Boom's story again (located at the beginning of each session). What lessons about forgiveness have you learned from her story?

To Be Like Jesus

As a Christian, your heart's desire should be to please God, to obey the instructions found in His Word and reflect the character of Christ. Whether you're a new Christian or you've been walking with the Lord for many years, forgiveness is tough. About the time you've forgiven your offenders, another situation will come up where you need to forgive—and likely someone will need to forgive you again.

The process of needing to receive forgiveness and to extend forgiveness is ongoing and seemingly endless. Whether you need to receive or extend forgiveness, both are possible because of Christ. He freely and willingly offers His unconditional forgiveness. He sweeps away all your offenses.

"I have swept away your offenses like a cloud,
your sins like the morning mist."

Isaiah 44:22

Joseph: An Example of Forgiveness[15]

What could erupt in more resentment than jealousy and friction within the family? Consider the story of Joseph in Genesis 37–45. Joseph could have chosen to be vindictive, yet was forgiving.

Joseph is the youngest and favorite son of his father, Jacob. His eleven older brothers are so bitter and jealous that they throw him in a pit, sell him into slavery, fake his death, then lie to their father, telling him Joseph has died. Later, Joseph is falsely accused of attempted rape, unjustly imprisoned, and forgotten by a friend who promises to help. Joseph has every reason to sever ties with his brothers, vent hatred on humanity, and slam the door on God, but he doesn't.[16]

Later, Joseph becomes the prime minister of Egypt, and a severe famine plagues the land. But God's involvement in Joseph's life while in Egypt has prepared him well. When his brothers hear of Egypt's abundance, they make a long journey from Canaan to obtain food. While in Egypt, they encounter their brother Joseph, whom they wrongly thought was dead. He is not. Joseph is the prime minister!

What a perfect opportunity for Joseph to take revenge! But instead of settling the score, Joseph speaks kindly to his brothers and recounts the way God used their treatment of him for his good, for their good, and for the good of the Egyptian people. Instead of being vengeful, Joseph forgives his brothers. (Read the amazing conclusion to Joseph's story in Genesis 50:15–21.)

"But Joseph said to them,
'Don't be afraid. Am I in the place of God?
You intended to harm me, but God intended it for
good to accomplish what is now being done,
the saving of many lives.'"

Genesis 50:19–20

Write from the Heart

Joseph made an important choice. He chose to forgive rather than be vindictive. Think of a situation where you chose to be forgiving rather than vindictive, or where you were vindictive rather than forgiving. What was the result of the choice you made?

The Parable of the Unmerciful Servant

In Matthew 18:23–35, Jesus tells a parable about a servant who owes the king 10,000 talents (millions of dollars in today's currency). The king orders the servant and his family to be sold, along with all they own. The servant falls on his knees and begs for mercy. "I will pay back everything," he says. The king extends mercy and forgives the entire debt.

The king represents our heavenly Father, who forgives all of our debt of sin when we sincerely come to Him for forgiveness and mercy (vv. 23–27).

Later this same servant grabs one of his fellow servants who owes him a hundred denarii (a few dollars). He chokes him and demands repayment. His fellow servant falls to his knees and begs for mercy, "I will pay you back." Instead, the first servant refuses to forgive and has the man thrown in prison until he can pay the debt. The servant who had his debts removed was not willing to forgive the debts of another servant who sought forgiveness (vv. 28–30). He refuses to forgive (v. 30).

When the other servants see what has happened, they are greatly distressed and tell the king about it. The cruel servant is called by the king, who is angered that his servant has not extended the same mercy he himself received from the king. The servant is then thrown in jail to be tortured until he can pay all he owes. Jesus concludes the story with a stern warning . . .

"This is how my heavenly Father will treat each of you unless you forgive your brother or sister from your heart."

MATTHEW 18:35

Don't get lost in the warning. Jesus is not teaching that we earn God's forgiveness by forgiving others or that we lose God's forgiveness if we don't forgive others. God's forgiveness is a free gift of grace based on the shed blood of Christ (Ephesians 1:7). The point of the parable is found in verse 33, where the king says to the servant, "Shouldn't you have had mercy on your fellow servant just as I had on you?" (Matthew 18:33). The servant was forgiven far more than his fellow servant, yet he refused to extend forgiveness. He went even further than refusal; he choked his fellow servant and threw him in jail. He demanded payment from him. It was not that the servant struggled to forgive his fellow servant but that he actively refused to forgive. He should have extended the same mercy he had received.

> "But because of his great love for us,
> God, who is rich in mercy, made us alive with Christ
> even when we were dead in transgressions—
> it is by grace you have been saved."
>
> EPHESIANS 2:4–5

This parable teaches many lessons about God's mercy, forgiveness, and grace. It's a reminder that a proper understanding and practice of forgiveness begins with receiving God's forgiveness.

While forgiveness can be a struggle, God still desires that we forgive. Understanding the struggle we would all have, God left frequent reminders in His Word of His forgiveness toward His people. And there is certainly no greater reminder than the cross. As we pursue forgiveness in our lives, we must always remember the precious currency that purchased our own forgiveness—the shed blood of Christ.

Write from the Heart

Read Matthew 18:23–35. What does this parable teach you about forgiveness? What are the differences between the king and the servant? How did the servant's actions fail to reflect true forgiveness?

Discussion/Application Questions

1. Over the past six sessions, how has your understanding of forgiveness changed as the result of this study? What are one or two key takeaways the Lord has revealed to you about forgiveness?

   ....

   ....

   ....

   ....

   ....

   ....

2. Forgiveness begins with the understanding that God completely forgives you for all your sins on the basis of the death and resurrection of His Son, Jesus Christ. Who in your life doesn't know about God's forgiveness? What steps will you take to make sure they learn about it?

   ....

   ....

   ....

   ....

   ....

3. Reflect for a moment on the ultimate price Christ paid for your forgiveness. He calls you to forgive because you have been forgiven. He calls you to pray for those who have mistreated you. Looking forward, how will you pray for those you need to forgive?

....

....

....

....

....

....

....

4. Psalm 103:2–3 says, "Praise the LORD, my soul, and forget not all his benefits—who forgives all your sins." As a prayer of thanksgiving and praise, write out your gratitude to God for His forgiveness.

....

....

....

....

....

....

Notes

Notes

"*You, Lord, are forgiving and good, abounding in love to all who call to you.*"

Psalms 86:5

Endnotes

1. Corrie ten Boom, John L. Sherrill, and Elizabeth Sherrill, *The Hiding Place* (Washington Depot, CT: Chosen, 1971); Corrie ten Boom and Jamie Buckingham, *Tramp for the Lord* (Fort Washington, PA: Christian Literature Crusade, 1974); Corrie ten Boom, *I'm Still Learning to Forgive* (Wheaton, IL: Good News Publishers, 1972).

2. Ten Boom, *I'm Still Learning to Forgive.*

3. Robert Jeffress, *When Forgiveness Doesn't Make Sense* (Colorado Springs, CO: WaterBrook, 2000), 47–49.

4. Jeffress, *When Forgiveness Doesn't Make Sense*, 46–51.

5. John Nieder and Thomas M. Thompson, *Forgive & Love Again: Healing Wounded Relationships* (Eugene, OR: Harvest House, 1991), Jeffress, *When Forgiveness Doesn't Make Sense*, 107–23.

6. David A. Stoop, *Real Solutions for Forgiving the Unforgivable*, Real Solutions Series (Ann Arbor, MI: Vine, 2001), 69–82.

7. Lawrence J. Crabb, Jr., *Understanding People: Deep Longings for Relationship*, Ministry Resources Library (Grand Rapids: Zondervan, 1987), 15–16; Robert S. McGee, *The Search for Significance*, 2nd ed. (Houston, TX: Rapha, 1990), 27–30.

8. Ten Boom and Buckingham, *Tramp for the Lord*, 181.

9. Lewis B. Smedes, *Forgive and Forget: Healing the Hurts We Don't Deserve* (San Francisco, CA: Harper & Row, 1984), 21–26.

10. Smedes, *Forgive and Forget*, 23.

11. David Augsburger, *The Freedom of Forgiveness*, rev. and exp. ed. (Chicago: Moody, 1988), 44–46.

12. Smedes, *Forgive and Forget*, 31–37.

13. W. E. Vine, *Vine's Complete Expository Dictionary of Biblical Words*, *electronic ed.*, s.v. "love" (Nashville: Thomas Nelson, 1996).

14. Ten Boom, Sherrill, and Sherrill, *The Hiding Place*, 238.

15. Robert Jeffress, *Choose Your Attitudes, Change Your Life* (Wheaton, IL: Victor, 1992), 102–7; see also Chuck Swindoll, "I Am Joseph!" *Insight*, Winter 1986, 3–9.

16. Jeffress, *Choose Your Attitudes, Change Your Life,* 102.

HOPE FOR THE HEART
Biblically Based Studies on Everyday Issues
6-Session Bible Studies

CHOOSING FORGIVENESS
Learn how you can be an expression of God's grace by forgiving others and find the freedom He intended you to have.
ISBN: 9781628623840

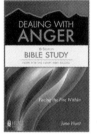

DEALING WITH ANGER
Have you ever reacted rashly out of anger—and lived to regret it? You can learn to keep your anger under control and learn how to act rather than react.
ISBN: 9781628623871

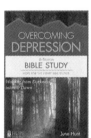

OVERCOMING DEPRESSION
Can anything dispel the darkness of depression? The answer is yes! Let God lead you through the storm and into the light.
ISBN: 9781628623901

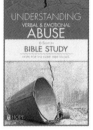

UNDERSTANDING VERBAL AND EMOTIONAL ABUSE
You can learn biblical truths and practical "how to's" for stopping the pain of abuse and for restoring peace in all your relationships.
ISBN: 9781628623932

HANDLING STRESS
Discover biblical approaches to handling stress. God wants to be your source of calm in stressful situations.
ISBN: 9781628623963

FINDING SELF-WORTH IN CHRIST
Learn to leave behind feelings of worthlessness, and experience the worth you have in the eyes of your heavenly Father.
ISBN: 9781628623994

www.HendricksonRose.com • www.AspirePress.com